# HOW TO TRAIN
# YOUR HUMAN

# HOW TO TRAIN YOUR HUMAN

## A CAT'S GUIDE

# BABAS

TRANSLATED BY KATHERINE GREGOR

ILLUSTRATIONS BY ANDREA FEROLLA

## HarperVia

*An Imprint of HarperCollinsPublishers*

HOW TO TRAIN YOUR HUMAN. Copyright © 2022 Giunti Editore S.p.A.,
Firenze-Milano, www.giunti.it. English translation copyright © 2024 by
Katherine Gregor. All rights reserved. Printed in the United States of
America. No part of this book may be used or reproduced in any manner
whatsoever without written permission except in the case of brief quotations
embodied in critical articles and reviews. For information, address
HarperCollins Publishers,
195 Broadway, New York, NY 10007.

HarperCollins books may be purchased for educational, business, or
sales promotional use. For information, please email the Special Markets
Department at SPsales@harpercollins.com.

Originally published as *Come addomesticare un umano* in Italy in 2022 by
Giunti Editore.

FIRST HARPERVIA EDITION PUBLISHED IN 2024

Designed by Yvonne Chan
Illustrations by Andrea Ferolla

Library of Congress Cataloging-in-Publication Data has been applied for.

ISBN 978-0-06-333648-3

24 25 26 27 28  LBC  5 4 3 2 1

CV 01.29.2024 0446

*To Prince Leopoldino, to Captain Fracasse, to Pimlico,*

*to Bobo, to Diego, to Luigino, to Pongo, to Amelia, to Marta,*

*to Bicia, to Tigre, to Popò, to old Mao, to Micione, to Little*

*Dorrit, to Apida, to Balletta, to Nòcciola, to Obama,*

*to Pastis, to Lion, and to all the cats who have deigned*

*to give us their friendship and consideration.*

# CONTENTS

# INTRODUCTION

We live on a planet infested with humans, who have altered it according to their image and likeness.

Survival is no mean feat: it's a hard world out there.

But when the going gets tough, the tough get going. There have never been so many humans on Earth, or so many cats.

It seems evident that we know how to coexist with these creatures, whose astonishing abilities are often guided by the most unfathomable stupidity.

The truth is that they are actually quite simple to train, and individually, some of them aren't all that bad.

What we propose to do in this manual is to provide a few tips on how to choose, train, and educate your human.

# 1

## HUMANS

## A FEW GENERAL NOTES ON THE SPECIES

Humans belong to the family of great apes. It's not their fault.

Like many primates, they are lively, noisy creatures equipped with prehensile front paws. In this species, the hind paws are partly atrophied through the bipedal position they insist on assuming.

They are large animals, oblong in shape, with no tail, and usually clumsier than other apes; they have a mane, especially developed in females, but otherwise they have no fur except in the most preposterous areas of their bodies.

Their muzzle is flat, though not unattractive, and the only characteristics that suggest anything vaguely feline are the frontal eyes; they have a large, practically useless nose and ears that do not move. The male of the species has whiskers, which it cannot, however, use.

The most successful parts of their bodies in a technical sense are their front paws or hands. These are equipped with long fingers with inconsequential claws and can move with extraordinary dexterity. They can look impressive to us and almost seem like animals with lives of their own, but they are tools that combine strength and precision, and once your specimen is trained, you will realize the countless advantages a couple of human hands at your service can bring you.

The most noticeable characteristic of these bipeds is that their bodies are coated with *things* that adhere to them like a second skin and—you will discover with horror—are in fact sometimes someone else's skin.

They have things they put on their heads, things that go in front of their eyes, and things that dangle from their bodies. On occasion, the females of the species slip their hind legs into things that make even the most basic motion difficult, and when they leave their dens, they carry with them so many things that they require special containers called handbags.

As you can easily guess, all these add-ons, which cling to them and make them heavier, do nothing to lessen their clumsiness.

We will call this human obsession with things *thingitis*.

*Thingitis* occupies a huge proportion of these creatures' lives, and we will frequently return to this topic.

Even though their appearance arouses suspicion, humans should not be underestimated. They can be extraordinarily intelligent, and we are not embarrassed to admit that many of their abilities are still a mystery to us. They are capable of altering their habitat and creating unexplainable phenomena like fire, light, canned tuna, and other wonders.

Humans communicate with their bodies just like other animals, but like birds, they also communicate verbally, in a constant, obsessive way.

It has been observed that their two levels of communication—corporeal and vocal—can even directly contradict each other. They can, for instance, greet one another warmly with verbal statements of affection, while their bodies express annoyance and hostility; at the same time, they can flatter you verbally and promise you food, while in actual fact they are planning to catch you and shut you up in a carrier.[*]

It's important to remember this duplicity, typical of the species, partly because—as it is not a feline characteristic—it is likely to take you by surprise time and again, as though for the first time.

Humans are social animals who live mostly in family groups.

When cubs reach sexual maturity, they sometimes leave their original nucleus to join small, young packs who share a single den.

Over the years, they tend to seek a mate and build a family, but not always. There are also solitary in-

---

[*] *Carrier*: a mobile jail for transportation.

dividuals, and those are often more inclined to be trained.

Some specimens spend most of their lives in their dens, which are large, comfortable, and highly desirable. Others are mostly outside procuring food and return at sundown. They are, above all, daytime hunters.

They are restless creatures and, once in their dens, are almost constantly engaged in activities consisting in handling and looking at things. We can state without a doubt that eyesight and touch are these mammals' most important senses, and some believe that this may partly explain our success with them.

According to some theories, the purpose of tools was once to make the lives of humans easier. There are oral traditions that date back to the times when these primates lived in caves and a flint dagger or spear was their trusted ally and could save their lives. Nowadays, the roles are reversed: humans are at the service of objects and take care of hundreds and thousands of things.

We don't wish to risk boring you with too many

technical notions at this time, but take just one typical example: eating.

Even such a theoretically simple operation becomes a triumph of *thingitis*.

Food often arrives in the den already *thingied*—or un-recognizable. All chopped up and sealed inside objects that require complex procedures to extract it, particularly for those without opposable thumbs.

Once caught, every chunk of food is handled, altered, cut up even more, heated, seasoned—in other words, ruined. This process involves a series of operations, a considerable amount of time, and many items of various shapes and sizes, some of them noisy, many a source of danger.

After they have ruined the food, humans take it to a table,[†] which they have laid with various objects,[‡] and

---

[†] *Table*: a small, raised reproduction of a floor.

[‡] *To lay the table*: a kind of ritualistic dressing of a stage for the food.

from there they lift it to their mouths exasperatingly slowly, using various other items that are the descendants of the aforementioned flint dagger.

This operation is constantly interrupted by verbal communication, drinking, and other distractions.

After feeding, humans require once again a lot of time to remove, wet, rub, and dry every single item they have used, in accordance with a long and complex ritual. There's a wide range of objects, like the dishwasher,[§] created expressly for this purpose: to take care of other objects that are constantly in use.

In practice, owing to *thingitis*, a process such as feeding, which would normally take a couple of minutes, can take up to several hours. Most of a human's life is spent taking care of its things, moving them, washing them, looking at them, and talking into them. Perhaps the meaning of *thingitis* could be attributed to the fact

---

§ *Dishwasher*: a cabinet that swallows objects and spits them back out after bashing them about noisily and removing food residue from them.

that human life is very long, and they don't know what to do with it.

It's no use denying that the human species is the world's most harmful and dangerous. Because of their large number—as well as other reasons—humans have made almost every habitat uninhabitable for other species. That's why carving out a corner for one's survival, often in the actual den, is an achievement. To be at their side is the only way to survive in a world dominated by humans. In truth, we are a notch higher, but let's not rub it in.

Some believe that however much we can like humans, and even grow attached to them, we must remember that they will always be wild animals: unpredictable and potentially dangerous.

We, however, are of the opinion that the right human, if well trained, can be an affectionate, loyal companion worthy of our trust—as long as it does not step too close to our paws.

———

## HISTORICAL NOTES

By the time the first humans appeared, cats had been ruling the planet for eons.

At first, these humans were viewed with contempt: they were just small packs of nomadic primates who would sporadically cross the territories of our ancestors, dig up roots, pick plants, steal small prey from us, then leave just as they had arrived.

Eventually, they learned to organize themselves into larger groups, became more skilled hunters, and started settling more or less permanently in dens.

Once they became sedentary and began stockpiling large amounts of food supplies, their interest in us grew increasingly noticeable.

We do not know who first had the brilliant idea of domestication, but it is almost certain that, once eye contact was made, it can't have been very hard to subjugate the ape. Domestication techniques are no doubt the same now as they have been since the dawn of time, and if they have changed, it's not in any significant way.

The best corroborated theory is that the first human to be domesticated was a female. The females of the species are in fact more sensitive, more intelligent, and quicker learners. It's also interesting to note that a newborn human baby is about the size of a cat. Maybe that's partly why mothers show such deep attachment to their cubs: they remind them of cats.

The devotion of this species toward us has gone as far as considering us divine. Divinity is a concept we felines struggle to comprehend. Can you imagine a mother cat who is omnipotent and immortal? This may give you an approximate idea of its definition.

Apparently, in ancient Egypt, in Mesopotamia, and in India, as well as in the Mediterranean, early human societies were matriarchal, worshipped the Mother Goddess, and idolized us as divine animals. Siamese cats have also been considered sacred in Thailand, as have Birman cats, otherwise known as "sacred cats of Burma."

The best-known case is that of the Egyptian goddess Bastet, the actual personification of the Mother Goddess in her gentlest, most maternal form, represented by a human body with a cat's head.

Back in those days, in Egypt, mummification—a horrifying practice of preserving the dead bodies of important persons or those considered divine—was very much in vogue. When the family cat died, it was customary also to kill the human closest to it, mummify it, and bury it together with the feline, so that the human could keep serving him or her in the afterlife.

This custom has been forgotten in human culture, so the poor souls believe the practice was the other way around and that it was the cat who was killed to keep the deceased human company. As though it weren't blatantly clear that the goddess Bastet had the head of a cat and not the reverse.

The fact that humans have often likened us to divinities has also had its downsides, particularly in the Middle Ages. Male humans, who paradoxically called themselves "the Holy Inquisition," hated human females and cats, especially black ones, and would hunt them down, torture them, burn them alive, and slaughter them in all kinds of ways.

The only upside was that, after millions of cats were exterminated, rats brought the Black Death, which killed twenty million primates.

Over time, the relationship between felines and humans has had its ups and downs, with its climax in ancient Egypt and its rock bottom in the Middle Ages, in the city of Vicenza, where it seems even now a wild fringe of the population still feed on feline flesh.

In any case, it has been a long association, with a history that has yet to be written.

## TRAINING AND DOMESTICATION

There are different levels of training.

The most basic level—let's call it elementary—consists in having food brought to agreed-upon locations, usually by a female of the species. This practice does not require special expertise, but neither does it guarantee continuity or, above all, quality.

What we consider a more advanced level, as referred to in this manual, consists in training to perfection one or—even better—several humans, by taking possession of their territory, becoming the absolute monarch, and getting them to wait on us hand and foot.

A dazzling example of the heights to which we aspire is provided by Prince Leopoldino, a cat of extraordinary beauty and intelligence who, with just one look, can prompt one of his apes to open a door, fetch a packet of kibble, or turn on a source of running water, depending on his whim.

This is the spirit we wish to impart to our pupils.

## CHOOSING A HUMAN

If you are born in a human den, you will be sharing it with humans that have already been partly trained by your predecessors. The simplest thing is to choose the weakest-willed individual to be the food dispenser, and the one you like best to be the love dispenser. So much the better if they happen to be one and the same.

But if you were born free and decide that the time has come to "get a human," then we suggest you examine all your options carefully before making your choice.

Use all your senses and your spirit of observation to

analyze possible candidates and thoroughly investigate their living conditions.

Take them into serious consideration only if they match most of these characteristics.

The ideal human owns prime territory.

By that we mean an extensive habitat with a portal to the outside world. If it's in a city,[¶] then it will have access to rooftops or a large garden or terrace. If it's located in the countryside, by the sea, or in the mountains, it will equally have easy access to the outside world.

The ideal human is a skillful hunter who brings excellent prey back to the den. Its social status is solid, its territory vast and rich in treats and beds.

The ideal human does not already belong to other cats. Or, if it does, it has belonged to your family for generations.

---

¶ *City*: a solid agglomeration of human dens—see *Habitat*.

The ideal human is not alone. However affectionate it may be, a loner cannot compete with the efficiency of an entire entourage. What if it falls ill? A couple is better.

The ideal human has no cubs, so that it can devote itself fully to your needs.

The ideal human is a female. They are quick learners and more dependable nurturers, although even a male, as long as it is sensitive and intelligent, will do.

There are other characteristics, but these tend to be connected more to education, something you can influence personally.

A blanket example: the ideal human idolizes and respects you; it does not take advantage of its brute force and gigantic size to scoop you up in a coercive embrace.

## 2

SEDUCTION

## COURTSHIP

Once you have identified your ideal candidate, move on to the conquest phase.

It's important to bear in mind that humans are seriously impaired when it comes to the senses. Anything that concerns smell, secretions, and such is totally wasted on them; if anything, it could be counterproductive. When it comes to the sixth sense and the perceptions they call "extrasensory," they've got nothing. They can cross energy fields, cosmic meridians, and ghosts without realizing it. In your commands, you must therefore focus on sight, touch, and hearing—although that, too, is barely developed.

The first contact will be visual: you should show yourself to the human and signal that you have seen it.

If you have made the right choice, the mere fact that you are dignifying it with your attention should propel it into a state of excitement.

## THE LOOK

The look is the first step and benchmark of seduction.

- Catch your human's eye.
- Squint slightly.
- Look at something else, pretend you've lost interest.
- Lick yourself nonchalantly.
- Look at the human again.
- Squint slightly.
- Look away.
- Stretch lazily.
- Yawn.
- Look into its eyes.
- Etc.

Remember not to look at it for a protracted time: these creatures cannot hold our gaze for too long. But do it often, furtively, from over your shoulder; when you wish to move on to a more advanced level, you will look at it with your head cocked.

How will you know if the look is working? First of all, the primate will look back at you. It may bare its teeth and crinkle its muzzle into a snicker, which, in its language, expresses pleasure. Sometimes, it squats. It's also likely to make sounds at you.

## PURRING

An effective technique in body-to-body contact is purring. For some reason, possibly connected with sound frequency, apes are crazy about it. It makes them happy and proud: knowing that we are enjoying their company increases their satisfaction and probably an especially fragile human feeling called self-esteem.

Purring must be used with abundance and generosity, and it will provide the sound basis for other seduction techniques.

## VOCAL CALLS

Gentle meowing is a powerful call for the well-disposed ape.

The softer and more childlike your sounds, like a kitten, the better.

The meowing must be delicate and hesitant, love calls emitted in a submissive tone. Also try blending purring with meowing by creating a kind of "rrrrmeow" sound.

Do not overuse vocal calls. Save them. You need them to attract attention, but once the attention is obtained, move on to nonverbal language such as looks, purring, affectations, and displays.

This vocalizing during the seduction phase will be very different from the more modulated and ultimately formidable, relentless screams you will use later on, when you want to shake up the primate's sluggish conscience to impose your iron will.

## AFFECTATIONS

Once you have displayed your *distance* seduction repertoire, it's time to move on to out-and-out affectations.

Affectations involve physical contact and, in their classic form, consist in rubbing yourself against the human's legs, lingering there while your body vibrates against them, then giving them one final caress with your tail before walking past them. Then you will immediately turn around, go back, and repeat the process on the other side. Naturally, all this must be accompanied by glances, purring, and soft vocalizations.

This process must be repeated an unspecified number of times: the aim is for the subject to melt, lean down to stroke us, start to emit vocal calls in return, and in its most macroscopic expression, progress to the "voicey-woicey," a phenomenon we will explore shortly.

The next level of affectation requires reaching up to the primate's muzzle by climbing onto an appropriate support and repeating the aforementioned maneuver—only this time, instead of acting on the legs, you rub yourself against the creature's chest, arms, and muzzle. This way, you will find yourself muzzle to muzzle for the first time: a moment of reciprocal trust crucial to the taming process.

If you are highly skilled, it is the human that will stoop and squat on the ground so that the affectation can take place muzzle to muzzle. Of course, this also depends on the human. It could take years or happen from the start. If it's an elderly specimen or one who is unable to squat because of other physical impairments, it will be up to you to find a technique for reaching its muzzle. If it's sitting, climbing on its lap will do.

## DISPLAYS

Now that you've kindled the fire of love in your human, keep it burning.

In order to do that, you must display your beauty before it.

Walk: show it how it's done. Sit: show it how it's done.

Yawn: show it how it's done by revealing all your little brilliant-white fangs, your curled tongue, and the intriguing pattern on the roof of your mouth.

Stretch: show it how you stretch from the end of your paws to the tip of your tail. Stroll before it while it's sitting at the table, busy looking at or handling things. Lie down lazily where it can't fail to see you. Curl up like a doughnut. Sprawl like a sea lion in the sun. Squat like a sphinx, paws together. Show yourself full-face and in profile; strut around with your tail like a question mark; lie on your side on the floor and arch your back like a parenthesis.

Then, once you're ready to administer the final blow: roll over, lie down belly up, retract your front paws like a bunny rabbit, and spread your hind legs, revealing your furry tummy. Now roll to your right and left while *looking* at the human.

If it wants to touch your tummy, resist any possible instinct to run away and allow it, still rocking from side to side.

If it touches your muzzle, nest your head in the palm of its hand and keep it there while emitting mighty purrs.

Unless the human is defective, at this stage it should be yours.

## Folly Olympics

These are different from pure displays of beauty. They are moments when you're overwhelmed with feline folly and yield to it: running around the house like crazy; climbing, enraptured, on furniture and curtains; taking prodigious leaps for no apparent reason; and savaging inanimate objects.

This physical prowess usually triggers in humans an adrenaline rush that rekindles their adoration for us.

## RITUALS

Rituals formalize and strengthen the relationship. Use your creativity to establish daily or at least regular habits to share with your primate.

This could be an afternoon nap or an evening stroll around the house; any regular shared activity will do, but an original one's better.

The famous Luigino da Poponaia, a ginger tom from Lake Como venerated by generations of humans, would climb on the table every morning when the alpha female of the household was about to feed. He would grab her attention with a paw, which he would then rest on that of the creature, in a position called "hand in hand," throughout the whole process—rendering the feeding considerably longer and more complicated than it would have been otherwise, given the primate's now-limited use of its extremities.

The alluring and fearsome Bicia, the Gray Kitty, would rush over whenever she heard the theme of *Born Free*: the story of Elsa, a lioness who adopts a couple of humans in South Africa. She ignored all other TV programs but never missed an episode of this series, which she would watch from her place of honor on the arm of the couch with the rest of the family.

These rituals will secure an everlasting spot in these creatures' hearts and will be remembered and sometimes passed on to posterity.

## INTIMACY

Once you've hooked your human, you can frolic with it: physically jump on it, trample on it, walk all over it. It will love this. Seek regular physical contact.

Find a comfortable nook between its body and the couch it's sitting on and curl up there, partly on a foot in an unnaturally bent position, partly on its thigh.

Pretend to sleep, forcing it into an uncomfortable, painful position for hours on end.

If the ape's position allows it, place yourself on its chest, making it hard for the creature to breathe.

The lap is another area you must frequent regularly.

Once you've settled comfortably, you can start the kneading operation, pushing with your paws in a rhythmical fashion, unsheathing your claws and gently sinking them into the human's sweater or T-shirt,* or straight

---

* *Sweater, T-shirt*: manifestations of *thingitis*—layers of stuff that cover the human body and that are derived from plants or hair removed from other animals.

into its body—as long as you purr throughout and, if necessary, roll over slightly when the human looks at you, showing your state of well-being.

## DISAPPEARANCES

A good habit is sometimes to disappear by using the ancient feline magic that enables us to dissolve into thin air for a lapse of time, from a few minutes to several hours. We won't go into detail on disappearance techniques: all cats have known them since the dawn of time, and this is not the right forum to advertise them. We simply invite you to use them every now and then.

Make yourselves invisible and resist the temptation to show your presence, even when the human's calls to you grow increasingly frantic and emotional.

A smidgeon of melodrama is highly beneficial to the passion of the primate.

## The Voicey-Woicey Phenomenon

A mark that your seduction endeavor is successful is the "voicey-woicey."

These are baby sounds emitted by the ape that are especially unpleasant, high-pitched, and persistent. Adults usually produce them around cubs of their own or other species. It is believed that humans emit them when overwhelmed with love. The voicey-woicey generally comes with senseless phrases, often padded out with nonexistent words, like "Whose sweetie-weetie is this?" or "Whose pawsies are these?"

In extreme cases, the voicey-woicey utters distorted sentences, such as "Whose teeny pawsies are zese?" and other atrocities too embarrassing to quote.

As a rule, the voicey-woicey heralds or accompanies the triumph of your seduction endeavor.

Naturally, you must never generalize: some humans use the voicey-woicey very easily, with any cub, animal, and at times even objects or plants, while others never do but can still express deep, faithful, and undying love for you.

# 3

# HABITAT

## THE HUMAN'S TERRITORY

Humans are social animals who flock in large communities; they live in colonies—countries, cities, apartment blocks—and often shift en masse in periodic migrations, especially during the warmer times of the year.

The average human lives in a den that can vary a lot in terms of size and comfort. There are also extreme cases of individuals who live in trailers, tree houses, or yurts. But what we're above all interested in are humans with a castle, a villa, or at least a penthouse.

As you will have gathered by now, whatever its appearance or dimensions, the den is cluttered with things: items of every shape and size, mostly not used but which nevertheless take up room. These hundreds or thousands of things are stored in pieces of furniture, which are larger objects. The remaining space for moving about in the den is therefore much reduced by *thingitis*.

When it comes to basic needs, the human habitat offers every convenience.

It contains several sources of water, although primates govern these arbitrarily.

There is an assortment of hiding places where humans keep deposits of food.

There is an abundance of heat sources in the winter and cool gusts in the summer.

Water, gas, and even human excrement flow from streams and other recesses concealed in the walls, and are sucked up by mysterious forces.

On human territory, you will always find a way to drink, eat, rest, and bury your droppings.

In some dens, you can also find a scratching post on which you can sharpen your claws. Alternatively, furniture can be used when necessary, although that often displeases the primates, who could then indeed turn against you.

Since humans have this biped mannerism, their lives mainly revolve around an altitude that oscillates between their genitals and their skull. Everything within that level is their kingdom, except for the bed where they sleep at night, which is usually lower down. Consequently, anything located below their knees and above their heads is hardly ever used.

The floor, with its landscape of tiles, timber, and above all, rugs, is available to us and offers limitless scale reproductions of the human apartment, with under-dens and possible hiding places under the furniture.

Thanks to larger pieces of furniture, it's also possible to get around at a higher altitude than that of the humans' domestic life. Climbing on bookcases and closets, as well as—for the bravest—curtains and lighting fixtures, allows you to combine a little healthy exercise with the fun of discovering new places and watching the den's activity from a privileged viewpoint.

The inside of furniture—closets, cabinets, and kitchen units—can have pleasant surprises in store: secluded bed space, food reserves, and valuable hiding places.

## BEDS

Beds—one of the most indisputable wonders so expertly created by humans for their world—deserve a separate chapter.

Cushions, baskets, chairs, couches: the primate's den is a comfort paradise.

The bed of all beds is the king-size bed, a large, stuffed area furnished with soft layers into which humans slide to sleep.

The king-size bed offers countless opportunities for entertainment:

- for leaping between the layers and excitedly arranging them whenever the bed is being made, an event you can always take part in;
- for sleeping and idling;
- for physical exercise and hunting the bulges that move beneath the surface, especially when these are at the level of the apes' hind legs;
- for hiding you from possible dangers or bothers, either under the soft layers or under the actual bed, whose width makes it hard for the apes to reach you even when they extend their paws;
- for vomiting when you're sick. Should the king-size bed be unreachable for some reason, you can always throw up on a couch, an armchair, or at worst, on a rug, as long as you avoid the bare floor and make sure you find some fabric, so much the better if it's expensive;
- for giving birth.*

---

* When humans showed Tigre the spot they had prepared for her imminent labor—a closet in a utility room (yuck!), she faked mild interest out of mere courtesy; then she gave birth comfortably on their king-size bed, as befitting her rank, giving life to the legendary Bobo and his sisters.

The next best thing to the king-size bed is the couch. The ideal habitat has several living rooms or at least several couches, so even if your primate wishes to entertain guests—an unfathomable activity the creatures are determined to practice—you will always be guaranteed your spot.

Still, the coziest bed will always be the one prewarmed by a human. Being restless creatures, they can never stay still for long; you must make sure to be in the vicinity and, as soon as the ape gets up, immediately take its place. When it comes back, pretend you're asleep. If it pushes you away, stick around and don't give up: wait for it to get up again.

According to Prince Leopoldino, the well-trained specimen prewarms the bed, stands up, walks away, and—if upon return it finds its previous seat occupied—gently moves away so as not to disturb you and finds itself another, cold chair.

Humans sometimes prepare beds especially for you, but these are usually not as comfortable as theirs. But do use them at least once or twice, if nothing else to let them know you appreciate their doing something for you.

Noteworthy makeshift beds also include stacks of clean, ironed laundry, always pleasant and fragrant, and the coats and handbags of guests, preferably those allergic to cats.

## BOUNDARIES

Like felines, humans are strongly territorial. Unfortunately, however, these mammals do not mark their territory with urine or other olfactory signals. Therefore, it is quasi-impossible to work out where a specimen's territory begins and ends, especially once you leave their den and are outdoors.

Consequently, you could witness apparently incomprehensible scenes: your primate getting agitated and emitting loud cries at you; presenting large amounts of food in an attempt to attract you; trying to follow you to rooftops, risking its own life; an unfamiliar primate and yours coming to blows.

All this could be connected to the fact that your human's terrace becomes at some point that of the neighbor or of the condo. It's not something especially worth worrying about: you will obviously go where you see fit in any case. Still, it's interesting to know.

On the other hand, this obsession with boundaries is also found inside the den, which is usually divided into airtight compartments. Between the different areas there's usually a *door*: a semimobile wall that either slides or swivels on a linchpin and is maneuvered with a protruding metal object halfway up called a *handle*; as the name suggests, it's made expressly for hands. Doors can suddenly attack us and sometimes move with no human intervention, slamming hard.

You will have a belligerent attitude toward doors.

Make it clear from the outset that you demand they always be kept open.

As a rule, park yourself in the doorway as often as possible.

If they insist on closing a door, start yelling loudly that you want to come in. Once inside, if they shut the door again, yell loudly that you want to go out. Repeat this procedure whenever necessary. The aim is to drive the primates to exhaustion, until they either leave the doors open or install smaller doors known as *cat flaps* for our exclusive benefit, through which you can go in and out whenever the fancy takes you.

If your humans are especially slow on the uptake, you'll have to learn to open the doors yourself.

The technique consists in jumping up, attacking the handle, and hanging off it with your full weight. The impact of the leap should be enough to shift it. If there are two of you, work as a team: one of you pounces on the handle, the other pushes the door.

If the door opens toward you, leap and hang off the handle, then give it a confident thrust of the hip. This is a more advanced technique, and if you can't manage it, you can always use a human.

The front door, which separates the ape's territory from the rest of the world, is especially important.

Whatever may lie beyond this door—be it a wild garden or an ordinary residents' staircase—make sure you can get past it and escape at the first opportunity.

In case it's a garden, take your time and come back only once you're tired of the inconveniences of the natural world.

If, on the other hand, there are just landings and stairs, flee anyway: run like crazy, as though your life depended on it, even if it's only for a few seconds, before you stop on the upstairs landing.

This may sound like a senseless act, but it isn't.

It can guarantee you food.

Prince Leopoldino, for instance, trained his primates like this: no sooner does he step over the threshold and shoot up the stairs than the duty ape, upset by the flight of its beloved, runs to fetch the box of kibble and shakes it like a maraca in a desperate attempt to call him back. Only then does the prince condescend to return to his estate to enjoy his snack.

Not everybody is as skilled as he is, and you may not be able to obtain food that way.

But it does make it clear that you cannot be taken for granted. It's important to frighten them and make them believe they could lose you unless they make cohabitation truly irresistible for you.

Unlike doors, windows mainly face the outside world. Since they are located at quite high altitude, they require a leap to reach them, and what's annoying is that until you land on the sill, you don't know exactly how wide your support area is or what lies beyond it. Prior to jumping, an in-depth study of the situation is of paramount importance; do not allow yourself to be teased by evil pigeons, and never get distracted where a window is concerned. Humans live in vertically stacked territories that can reach dizzying heights, and this may be the one instance in which they overestimate us: aware of our ability to land on all fours, they tend to underestimate the dangers of cornices, railings, and windowsills.

Sadly, there are countless victims of heights.

## Colonialism

If you've trained your human to let you in and out whenever you wish, you may entertain the prospect of colonizing other off-limit territories.

Returning to Luigino, the Lake Como ginger, he led a perfect, happy double life for some time, with two identities and double rations of beds, food, and cuddles. He would leave the den of his first adoptive family, walk down one flight of stairs, and enter straight into his second family's home. A very convenient arrangement.

One day, while engaged in *thingitis*, Ape No. 1 dropped a sock from the drying rack. She went to knock on the door of the neighbors on the floor below to retrieve it: imagine her surprise at finding Luigino comfortably settled on a throne prepared for him, dominating the living room, with other bowls, other worshippers, and another human name. Above all, imagine Luigino's surprise at seeing Ape No. 1 turn up unexpectedly—and uninvited—in Territory No. 2.

# 4

## COHABITATION AND HOUSE-TRAINING

## FOOD

Humans are unpredictable hunters. They sometimes leave the den for several days in a row and return empty-handed, and at other times pop out for a few minutes and come back laden with prey.

Their hunting methods are still a mystery to us. What's certain is that they conceal large quantities of food in their dens—foolishly, always in the same places—and get it out at prearranged times. There's one specific hiding place that's always cold and produces different marvels every time. As a matter of fact, they keep opening and closing it as though they, too, can't believe their eyes. This eternal source of delights is called a *refrigerator,* and it's advisable to be in the front row whenever it's opened.

Since they eat at prearranged times, they tend to want us to do the same. It's not easy to train them to provide food for us at any moment, but have faith: it is an achievable feat.

### Phase One

First and foremost, find the location where they've hidden your food: your objective is to lead them there, and for that, you'll resort to your entire seduction repertoire, from the look to a liberal use of affectations.

Begin the affectations in any spot of the den and, once you have the ape's attention, shift ever so slightly, one affectation after another, toward the food depository, until you're standing in front of it. At this stage, produce loud verbal calls and, if necessary, *mime* the act of eating, opening and closing your mouth silently.

There are those who believe in telepathic communication: sit with your paws together as close as possible to the source of food, stare at the human, and mentally convey to it the command "You will feed me." If the individual is especially receptive, this may work.

This repertoire is amply sufficient when dealing with a primate that's docile and eager to learn.

But let us imagine that the human is unwilling to follow you—that it's prey to *thingitis* and is intent on handling, looking at, or talking to objects.

In that case you will need more advanced techniques. Here they are, listed in order; if one doesn't work, move on to the next, more extreme one, and so forth.

1. Strut in front of them, perhaps walking on the items they are looking at or handling, signaling your urgency.
2. If it's an object equipped with a keyboard, scamper over it, pushing several keys at once in lethal combinations.
3. Sit in front of the ape and scream in its face.
4. If it pushes you away, continue to scream loudly in the vicinity.

5. If they shut a door between you, try to knock it down and persevere with the loud yelling. We know this is tedious, but in the long run it seems that vocal language is all this species can truly comprehend.

6. If there is an object the primate holds particularly dear (from a collection, something made of crystal or porcelain, a precision instrument essential for its activities, or the like), jump on it, making sure the primate notices.

7. If there are other cats or animals subordinate to you, like canines, for instance, this is the time to torment them until they complain raucously.

   This can be entirely staged, although it must be credible: Prince Leopoldino and his brother, the famous Captain Fracasse, enact furious rows with blood-curdling screams to rouse their ape from its stupor, a technique that works without fail.

8. As a last resort, if there's no one else to help you stage an attack, move directly to physical calls to the human in question. We tend not to use violence with

these poor beasts, but it is sometimes necessary. A light bite or a little blow with a half-unsheathed claw should suffice to rouse the primate, who will then get up, complain, and finally carry out its duty.

Let us conclude with a very ordinary scenario: imagine the human is fast asleep and you start feeling a little hungry. In that case, the techniques are basically as above, with a couple of variations.

Here is their order:

1. Call the human gently, meowing next to its ears (the atrophied little things on the sides of its head).
2. Sit on its chest and call it loudly and insistently, trying various registers.
3. Knock objects off the item of furniture next to the bed: if there's a glass of water, choose that.
4. Climb on an item of furniture near the bed and, from there, jump on the bed.

5.  Climb on an item of furniture near the bed and, from there, jump on the human.
6.  Hit another family pet (preferably on the bed).
7.  Hit the sleeping human—gently at first, then harder—from a shy tap on the nose to a full blow with a claw.
8.  Once the primate gets up, swaying, to fulfill its duties, run merrily between its feet and vocally express your enthusiasm. It is always important to let humans know that their efforts are appreciated.

## When They Are Eating

Humans generally eat at a table, and the process involves a consistent *thingitis*; the table is therefore full of objects. Get them used to leaving room for you. To begin with, this could be on one side, where they harbor the illusion that you can't reach the food. But you will gradually gain ground until you conquer the center of the table, where you can order morsels with looks, chatter, and if necessary, predatory blows with your paw.

An expert in this is Captain Fracasse, a huge black cat as heavy as a medium-size dog, who positions himself on the table as soon as his humans' mealtimes come. At first, he takes a spot on the side; then, slowly and almost imperceptibly, taking advantage of the apes' concentration on their food, he shifts until he is next to one of the humans, stretching his neck over the plate in a position they call "ox and ass."* But he maintains a show of indifference, as though the process were of no interest to him and he just happens to be there by pure chance. After a little while, once the humans have gotten used to his presence, he strikes.

He has two techniques: first, he stretches, lazily extending one of his paws toward the food, trying in this way to hook a piece of cheese or another food worthy of interest. It's a natural but slow movement, and for that reason the technique often fails. In this case, he initiates Plan B: he grabs the morsel with a swift movement of the paw.

---

* The myth of the *Nativity* includes the image of an ox and an ass, their large heads panting over a manger. This myth is enacted in the *Nativity Scene*, an amusement set up every winter especially for your entertainment, in lieu of or concurrently with the *Tree with Baubles*.

This attempt is also often unsuccessful, although the outcome is always positive; if all else fails, at the end of their meal, these humans, who are wonderfully well-mannered, give him some tidbits of their own free will.

During the training process, you will accept samples of various foods, even showing interest in vegetables, such as pumpkin, zucchini, string beans, and asparagus; you can show enthusiasm for olives, dairy products, certain meats, and fish. But only if this food originates from the table or from the hands of the humans.

You will not enjoy these same foods if they are put in your bowl. And here we come to the crux of this process: what we have outlined so far is only phase one of the training.

### Phase Two

The next phase is especially interesting: scornfully decline food, and not only when the menu is repetitive or of poor quality.

Every now and then, for the sake of principle, look with

disgust at what they're offering you and walk away indignantly. It will leave the primates confused and disheartened, and this will lead to a distinct improvement in your menu.

Prince Leopoldino, for example, spurns all sashimi except tuna and sea bass, which he loves. Salmon he views with indifference, and shrimp with annoyance. With some foods, he simply licks off the gelatin, and he shies away from others with a frightened leap. It works. Only prized morsels reach his jaws, and whenever his humans eat sushi, they order tuna and whitefish specially for him.

Your finickiness will become proverbial and will eventually turn into a challenge for humans: they'll be happy and proud when they find a food you visibly enjoy.

## REST

Humans are terribly hardworking and rest very little, mainly at night. It won't be easy to combine your natural rhythm with theirs.

By day, they are in the grip of unrestrained, senseless activity. They often seem tired, but instead of stopping for a catnap, in harmony with the rhythm of Mother Nature, they perk themselves up with liquid stimulants and continue fussing about until they collapse, once and for all, in the evening, after hours and hours of tireless exertion.

If they're outside the den during the day, you'll have all the time in the world to go from a wink to a nap, from a snooze to a siesta, with short breaks to nibble a little kibble, hunt geckos on the terrace or in the garden, or do some proper grooming.

Having some quiet rest could be more complicated if they are in the den: many of their activities are either noisy or devious. We believe the most odious one consists in moving around a large, screaming object that sucks the surface of the entire territory, without the least regard for the serenity of the residents. Unfortunately, no solution has been found to date to prevent our pets from indulging in this pastime.

In any case, it makes sense to fit in with their rhythm as much as possible, and even if at night you feel naturally sprightly and craving adventure, in a human den, that actually becomes the ideal time to rest.

Basic training includes resting on top of your specimen, preventing it from making any movement.

This can be done while the primate is sitting down, but it's even more comfortable when it's lying on what will become your favorite place, which you will generously share with it: the king-size bed.

Occupy the area when the biped lies down or, even better, just before it does; a clear sign of its intention is when it brushes its fangs.

Pick a central area and make yourself comfortable: it will be up to the primate to adapt and find a more peripheral position. At this stage, you can make yourself even more comfortable, exiling the ape or apes definitively to where they don't bother you too much. Any hollow in the human body—it has many, being long and full of sharp edges, like a large stick insect—is perfect for nestling: between its legs, behind a bent knee, against its belly, between the ankle and the foot, or if you wish, even on its head—as long as you cling to it physically, something that will send it into ecstasy.

If you can, it's considered standard practice to wait for the first light of dawn before waking it up and demanding breakfast.

## COMMUNICATION

Humans are typically song creatures, like birds, and emit an almost constant string of sounds.

At the same time, more or less consciously, they communicate nonverbally.

By living in close quarters with them, you'll learn to understand their intentions and, naturally, to distinguish a few sentences, words, and expressions in their funny language.

On no account must they realize this. It will give you a considerable advantage over them. First and foremost, it's convenient to know their plans in advance and, wherever possible, adopt the required countermeasures.

Do they mean to play some dirty trick on you, like administering poisons?[†] Are they planning on going away for a couple of days and leaving you to the unsatisfactory care of the ape downstairs?

To understand the importance of the code of silence, you just need to look at most dogs: they're totally subjugated.

If you show the primates that you understand their language, they may expect you to act accordingly and even get upset when that doesn't happen.

It has been demonstrated that the verbal communication of these creatures changes depending on their

---

† Your human will periodically administer to you small quantities of poison, which they call medicine, flea powder, or other made-up names.

geographical locations—a complication vaguely akin to the principle of doors between rooms, in other words the imaginary boundaries established by this species.

But it's important to speak several human languages only if you move in international circles.

Prince Leopoldino, for example, speaks three languages: Italian, English, and French. He is self-taught in the latter, so not as fluent in it as in the others.

Every now and then, humans "sing" and "dance." When they emit rhythmical sounds, howl, warble, or trill, rolling their eyes, it's called singing. When they fidget as though pursued by a swarm of wasps, skip on the spot, shake, sway, throw their limbs in every direction, and suddenly flop, it's called dancing. To you, these phenomena will seem incomprehensible and, most of all, genuinely embarrassing.

These are expressions of joy and vitality; as long as you keep out of the reach of their large paws while they dance, they are not dangerous.

## THE DEPRIVATION OF PRIVACY

Techniques of privacy deprivation are essential for strengthening your social position in the household and your dominion over humans.

Besides sleeping or pretending to sleep on top of your ape, here are other circumstances in which to parade your discreet but inescapable presence.

### In the Bathroom

Always come in to supervise exactly what it's doing. Refrain from expressing anything, as though you are not all that interested, but try always to be there, at least for a quick check.

When the ape happens to be in a vulnerable position—exiting the shower or sitting on the toilet—make sure you push the bathroom door wide open.

If your litter box is there, try to time your *defecatio* with their presence in the room, so they may fully appreciate its pungent odor; it's better to perform this when the ape is unable to escape.

## During Mating

If not too dangerous, be present exactly where this act takes place. In most cases, it occurs on the king-size bed, of which you will occupy a peripheral area.

Humans hugely complicate this simple practice, too, and before getting down to the actual mating get lost in a series of secondary, unfathomable activities. They feverishly change positions, and one gets the feeling they don't know exactly what they're looking for. Fascinating and entertaining as the process may appear to you, do not make your interest too obvious; you can slumber or give an absent-minded look every now and then, even though during some phases you can get closer for a better look, keeping a clinical, detached approach.

The most skilled trainer should be able to lounge on a bed where human copulation is taking place, confining the couple to the edge of the bed.

Needless to say, similar invasions of your privacy on the part of humans will be frowned upon and not easily tolerated.

## GIFTS AND REWARDS

Reward your human when it does something for you. It's important for it to learn to associate its efforts to please you with something nice: an affectation, a nose-to-nose contact with purring, a partial roll.

It will always be ready to repeat an action that leads to a reward.

On the subject of rewards, prepare yourself for some upsetting news: these mammals do not like being brought prey—the best gift a feline can give and receive.

A large, gutted lizard, a nice tail that's still flicking, or a decapitated little bird will create embarrassment, if not actual hysteria.

You can still bring them into the house with loud satisfaction, and even put them on the king-size bed as a surprise, as long as you're not disappointed by the humans' lack of gratitude.

This is especially puzzling, since these primates are omnivorous and most of them eat other animals—although cut into small pieces. It's therefore extraordinary to see them handle long-dead corpses daily, but when these are brought to them freshly killed—and in some cases still alive!—they react so absurdly.

The cat Ugo, a famous hunter, when still an adolescent, caught and killed a large crow. This was no mean feat; moreover, wedging the crow into the den through the cat flap was even more laborious.

When his primates came back home, they found a trail of blood across the hall. Following the trail in one direction, they reached the cat flap, where feathers and plumage had gotten stuck. Then they followed it in the opposite direction and came to the crow's body at the foot of the armchair, on which Ugo, exhausted and proud, was expecting their praise. His prowess was met with the usual cries of horror, and the older primate said, "If he brings us a crow while he's still a kitten, by the time he's an adult, we'll find schnauzers hanging from tree branches."

This is one case when the apes, in their own way, acknowledged a worthy enterprise. It is unlikely to receive any more acknowledgment than that.

## MIGRATIONS

This species periodically migrates, especially in the dry season.

We have already mentioned the importance of finding an animal with a large territory, with access to the outside world.

Some humans own various territories, one in the city and others in nature. To those of you who were born in cities, we unreservedly recommend the following solution: look for a primate who also owns properties to which to migrate or, as they put it, in which to take vacation.

However inconvenient the trip from one territory to another may be, it's usually worth enduring it without kicking up too much fuss because there are more opportunities for entertainment when on vacation. There are gardens, unfamiliar smells, waterways, bushes, herbs to eat and then vomit in the den, possible prey, and other cats; life in the open air is undoubtedly less tedious than in an apartment.

If anything, it's the prospect of returning to the city that will be boring, but by paying a little attention, you can pick up on the signals of preparation for the return and arrange not to be found when it's time to leave.

Migrations can last for a few days or else be of long duration.

Before migrating, humans always provide specific signals; one of them, unequivocal, is an explosion of *thingitis.*

A large number of items are pulled out of the furniture, moved, stacked in other places, and often looked at for a long time. Special self-propelling containers are extracted from closets and utility rooms, and filled with stuff the ape deems essential for its survival—even for as little as twelve hours away from its habitat.

You can sense agitation in the air, and activity grows even more frantic than usual; if several individuals inhabit the same den, they may start squabbling.

Once the items taken out of the furniture disappear into the self-propelling containers, it's time to set off.

Whenever human beings migrate, the situation often becomes—somehow or other—annoying.

If they leave without taking you with them, you could be left alone for most of the time, with the odd intrusion on the part of friends/relatives/others contracted to take care of your primary needs. On one hand, this means peace and quiet; on the other, the boredom of being on your own and shut in a confined environment could become overwhelming.

Alternatively, the den could be invaded full-time by other humans who take care of you and who, depending on the circumstances, can make themselves welcome or unpopular. These could be friends to whom your humans have lent the house, nephews or grandchildren, or permanent cat sitters.

In any case, this represents a change in habit, and like all change that hasn't been decided by you, it's a nuisance and, for the more sensitive among you, a source of stress.

If, on the other hand, you're involved in this phenomenon, the detestable carrier appears alongside the containers for human things.

Sometimes, the sly creatures don't take it out until the very last minute, so as not to upset you. At other times, even slyer creatures get it out days in advance, until you no longer pay attention to it—which is when they catch you and forcibly push you into the narrow cubicle.

The moment you're captured, we would advise you to fight and complain to make your disapproval clear; if, however, you have reason to believe that the migration could be beneficial for you in the long run by taking you to an agreeable place, do not overdo it with protests and, above all, act with dignity during the journey.

Hold back your discharges at all costs: traveling in your own feces never inspires the respect and admiration we want to instill in our humans.

Hysteria is not elegant either.

In this case, Captain Fracasse is a negative example.

Unlike his brother Leopoldino, Captain Fracasse is a naive creature. He never picks up on an imminent migration until he is slap-bang in the middle of one and experiences every one of them as a personal tragedy. He's docile when put in the carrier but then immediately opens his eyes wide and starts to emit chilling cries that are in no way feline. His quick succession of hoarse, powerful, and convulsive caterwauls loses its original nature and ends up resembling a mysterious sound, something between a donkey's braying and the barking of a large dog.

Having delicate nerves, Fracasse hates traveling alone, which is why his carrier is huge, since his brother travels with him.

The brother is usually cool and heroic, but when first caught, he, too, voices his indignation out loud, and during the first few minutes, they both push against the soft walls of the container, creating bulges that pop out now in the roof, now on the sides, now all over. A stranger might think that what's being transported is a wolverine or a pack of spider monkeys.

When humans carry them in the street, crowds of meddlers form around them; apes appear even at the windows and balconies, and the braver ones come close enough to ask what kind of creature is being transported.

The journey is usually by train: one of humanity's most unfathomable creations, a giant, noisy machine that swallows masses of creatures in one place and spits them back out in another. Trains are surprisingly comfortable on the inside, and once underway, Captain Fracasse pipes down; he's only prey to sporadic panic attacks, during which he pants, mouth and eyes wide open, like a fiend. He may emit on these occasions another sequence of fearsome cries, but then, exhausted, he falls into a deep slumber.

As you will have gathered by now, Prince Leopoldino and Captain Fracasse have a couple of exceptionally well-mannered primates at their disposal and so can afford to commit even such important *faux pas*.

Still, it's certainly not an example to follow.

Dignity, first and foremost.

### Narcotics

When it's time to migrate, some humans may try to administer narcotics to you to dull your senses and make you passive during transportation.

Try to spit them out. If you don't succeed, pretend to be dead.

Alternatively, fight the torpor with all your might, acting crazy. Humans will call this reaction, opposite to the desired outcome, a "paradoxical effect," and once you have gotten it into their simple little heads that you're too sensitive to tranquilizers (dead) or that you suffer from a paradoxical effect (crazy), they will immediately stop bothering you with drugs.

## HUMAN CUBS

However carefully you may choose your primate, one day they unexpectedly find themselves a mate and reproduce. No matter how alert you are, you are never totally safe from human cubs.

It is therefore important to mention them.

Cubs are dangerous rivals, and no sooner are they born than they hijack all the attention once reserved for you. There's not much you can do about it.

If you show annoyance or hostility, you will immediately be consigned to the status of pariah, with whole areas of the territory off bounds to you, and your social standing within the pack will be seriously compromised.

Having a friendly attitude toward them is the only way not to lose too many of your privileges.

One piece of good news is that for the first few months, human cubs are harmless. They are unable to move about independently or do anything except scream, eat, and defecate. Since, from the moment they are born, they are tightly wrapped in fabric stuff called *baby clothes*, they soil themselves with their own excrement; their parents clean them, then insist on bundling them again in other fabrics. The ensuing cycle proves the power of *thingitis* over humans from the moment they are born.

On the rare occasions when they are not all stained in feces, the little ones have an exquisite smell of milk.

During that time, they find it so hard to coordinate their movements that they could inadvertently hit you. Remain alert. There's nothing stopping you from sleeping on top of the cub, proving your passion for the creature, but make sure it also is asleep.

The most dangerous phase comes later, when they start crawling on all fours, a position in which they can be surprisingly fast. They grab things with their fat, prehensile little paws, which they cannot yet fully control. Subsequently, encouraged by the adults, they start walking with some difficulty, and that's when they suddenly—and frequently—fall.

This is the moment to educate them. It's during this stage that they can try clumsily to pick you up, hold you tight, squash your paws, yank at your whiskers, trap you in fabric things like the ones humans use, and actually *pull your tail*. And that is something you must never, for any reason, allow.

You will consequently always have to be vigilant. As soon as you detect this kind of unhealthy notion in the infant, we suggest the immediate emission of almighty screams of pain (even preliminary to the pain itself), so as to alarm the adults, followed by an immediate escape and a period of cautious distance from the subject.

The cub is untouchable, and you must not raise your paws to it unless the pain is unbearable. In that case, do not leave permanent marks.

A noteworthy exception is Bicia, the Gray Kitty, who had a particular intolerance for high-pitched sounds. Having grown up in a family with two human cubs, Bicia, whenever a child screamed, would come and smack it loudly. However, she could tell the difference between real cries of pain (such as when a cub stapled one of its fingers) and those connected with so-called tantrums, expressions of anger and frustration that use sound as their principal weapon; she would rush to it only then.

The time one of the cubs threw itself on the floor screaming and she bit its head is still remembered.

It was a totally understandable instinct: who among us has never experienced the irresistible desire to bite the head of a human cub who yells after dropping to the floor? The most extraordinary thing is that, while trying to push her away, the cub's parents were laughing (you know, when they bare their teeth with happiness?), and not only did the Gray Kitty not suffer the consequences of this clear aggression, but on the contrary, from then on she was viewed as a valuable ally in the education of their offspring.

Let us underline, however, that this is an exception. We are talking about primates trained by generations of cats and advise you against trying this with yours.

Cubs are untouchable, and remember that these mammals keep being so for a span as long as a cat's entire life and perhaps even longer. There are records of humans that are still fed and taken care of by parents who are old and staggering; these are extreme cases, but they do exist.

On the other hand, if you are lucky enough to be able to train a human from the time it's a cub, you could achieve brilliant results and earn yourself the best, most loyal companion anybody could hope for.

# 5

## HUMAN
## FIXATIONS

## THE BALL

You may run into a ball fanatic: there are many of them. These humans obtain or make a ball—a small, spherical object—and throw it at you. They expect you to catch it or hit it back toward them; they then remove it from you and start the game anew. At other times, they clumsily hide it and want you to find it.

If this does not bore you too much, kindly play along with them every now and then, and you will make them happy. These are innocent pastimes, usually of short duration because, however excited the primate might be by the exercise at first, it soon gets tired or else, as usual, distracted. If nothing else, by indulging it in this activity, you will help it keep active.

Going back to the Gray Kitty, the cub educator, she was a formidable athlete. Besides hitting little humans, she did not perform much physical activity. She therefore developed a genuine passion for this sport and was given regular workouts by her apes, who took turns throwing her compact aluminum balls to dizzying heights. Since they were especially playful individuals and desperate to show off, whenever visitors came to the den, the Gray Kitty was always summoned to carry out her exploits. Sometimes, she would actually be woken from a deep sleep with a request to exhibit her skills.

Depending on her mood at the time, she would decide whether to humor them.

Naturally, you are not obliged to submit to all their whims.

## THE KISS

A typical human expression of affection is the kiss. The ape extends its lips, which are remarkably mobile, and rests them on you—sometimes with a tiny act of suction and an irritating smacking sound.

Its huge head looms over you as it does this. Particularly if you're asleep, waking up to a giant creature stretched over your body smacking its lips on your head can be chilling. As if that were not enough, the ape could try to grab you and keep you still during the procedure and, in some cases, even *lift you to its mouth*. Although primates, whether domestic or wild, normally do not bite, we recommend you put up a fight and do not submit to these practices. Instead, encourage them to express their affection with rubbing, gentle scratching under your chin, or other, preferred methods, by setting an example.

If, however, you wish to spoil your biped, you may grant them the odd delicate kiss, but only when you show willingness.

### THE CAPTURE

Another expression of attachment that is characteristic of this species is capture. Every now and then, humans fall prey to an overwhelming instinct to catch us. They hold us tight in their long paws and, as mentioned in the previous section, may lift us to their mouths for a series of kisses.

In practice, they immobilize us and squeeze us against them. Sometimes, while holding us tight, they walk away and carry us to another part of the territory.

This often happens when strangers enter their habitat: the ape looks for, catches, and exhibits us.

Moreover, human cubs are great catchers.

The primate is very pleased when it captures us. Some cats enjoy this and cling to their great ape with real pleasure. Personally, I am not against being in close proximity to these creatures, but only when it is my choice.

## STEALING FECES

This is an embarrassing, murky page in the feline-human relationship. We are talking about the unfathomable habit this species has of rummaging through our litter box and removing its contents.

The human shows up more or less daily with a small shovel and digs in search of what we have patiently buried, then takes possession of it.

It steals balls of coated urine and feces, hides its treasure in a little bag, and takes it away.

Why? What does it do with it?

We don't want to know.

This means that, despite being small, the litter box is reusable. Some believe that's the reason for this bizarre habit: that it's purely an unselfish act of service. Maybe. We cannot rule anything out.


## BROODING

When you are resting on a table, a couch, or another piece of furniture, it may happen that the human places an item next to you that they clearly wish you to brood. Make sure you indulge them: it will be no effort for you and will leave the human overjoyed. This could be a remote control,[*] a cell phone,[†] or else a bunch of keys (less comfortable), a pen, or a book.

In any case, lie on said object without delay, making sure it vanishes completely under your body. After a while, the human will begin a ritual: it will get agitated and start looking around, as though searching for the item you are brooding. Only after a long time playing this pantomime will it try to retrieve the object, now warm, from under your body. Put up some passive resistance, trying, on this occasion, to weigh twice as much as usual.

If, when trying to repossess the thing you are brooding, it places another within your reach, quickly engulf it and begin a new brooding session.

---

[*] *Remote control*: the parasitical object of a larger object, the *television*, that captures these creatures' attention for hours on end.

[†] *Cell phone*: an object they worship and never part with.

## THE HORRIBLE MYSTERY

There is a very dark side to cohabiting with this species. One point no one can explain, but which carries reasonable doubt and is important to consider, is sudden and unjustified castration—or in the case of females, spaying—which cats who live with these primates inexplicably experience.

Nobody knows how it happens, but it is a fact that very few escape this fate. There are no firsthand testimonies of the procedure itself, and that makes everything even scarier.

What seems certain is that it's in some way the responsibility of one of the most terrifying human figures: the Untrainable, the Great Persecutor, the White-Clad, the Veterinarian.

Many of those who have experienced this fate remember the image of the Untrainable leaning over them—and then nothing else.

They woke up in their own den—or in some cases still

in the Untrainable's gulag—and everything had changed forever.

This barbaric practice is inexplicable. There is no doubt that these primates, in their own way, grow genuinely fond of us; it's therefore hard to believe that this procedure stems from a wish to harm us. And yet that is undeniably the result.

# 6

## COHABITATION WITH OTHER CREATURES

If you were born and brought up with other cats, you are familiar with the undeniable advantages offered by feline society—from sheer company to criminal conspiracies.

You can play, exercise, carefully groom one another, carry out plans difficult to see through on your own. And naturally, there's the joy of relationships and of sharing your life with your kind—especially if you love them.

The heroic Pongo, a mighty black cat who grew up in a household densely populated with humans and felines, had proclaimed himself champion of the oppressed. No matter what problems the other felines encountered, Pongo would come running at the first meow.

One day, the ginger Luigino stuck his head in a plastic bag and couldn't get it out: he ran around the house, terrified, bumping into furniture and residents until he crawled under a dresser, crying and asking for help.

The human family's cub rushed to rescue him and lay down under the dresser, trying in this uncomfortable position to free Luigino. Pongo arrived immediately, and his partial view of the situation clouded his judgment: thinking the cub had gone crazy and was trying to suffocate Luigino with a plastic bag, he attacked the cub. All hell broke loose under the dresser: Luigino was screaming, the cub was yelling, Pongo was bashing him. The other primates watching the scene were also shouting; in the end, they joined forces, managed to pull Pongo away, and shut him in another room. Luigino was freed, the wounded cub was treated, and Pongo was released from detention. He suffered no reprisal: he had clearly acted with noble intentions, and even the manhandled, bleeding cub respected him all the more for it.

In other circumstances, cohabitation with other cats may occur unexpectedly and suddenly: one fine day, your human comes home with another, without asking your permission.

You may have finally reached the age when one feels adjusted and calm, and here comes a crazy preteen.

Maybe you have just established a clear rapport of subordination in which the human has achieved optimal thoughtfulness, and then one day it arrives with two babies it can't take its eyes off.

Or, even worse, as you sit nonchalantly licking your paw on your favorite armchair, the door opens, and they bring into the household a middle-aged wretch, flea-ridden and scruffy, accustomed to brawls among street cats, who barely speaks your language. The hobo might be a female, a fury the primate insists on calling *kitty* and who swears like a trooper and yells death threats at you as soon as she's on the doorstep.

Anything can happen, so it's good to be ready.

The most important thing is to remember that, whatever they may be, they're still cats.

However tested by life, upset, ignorant, or filthy they might be, deep inside that disaster area still resides a kindred spirit, superior and longing to emerge and glow.

I know, it's hard to see it sometimes. But give it time

and have faith in the possible amazing transformation even in the worst flea-ridden beast.

## COHABITING WITH INFERIORS

### Plants

*Indoor Plants*
They can be divided into two categories: plants and cut flowers.

The latter must be ripped to pieces.

Start by attacking the receptacle, from which you could even try drinking, head-butting the flowers out of your way. Then rage against the buds by biting them and peevishly slapping them, then finishing them off by swiping them with your claws. Last, stage the grand finale by knocking the vase with the water over the vegetation graveyard you have thereby created.

Plants are in pots filled with soil and are arranged in the apartment in a way that enables you to dig inside them.

Trunks and leaves can be annihilated with various techniques you can explore to your heart's content, providing constantly new pastimes.

### Outdoor Plants

The plants on the terrace or in the garden offer good alternatives to the litter box.

Indeed, humans regularly spread on them what they call fertilizer—which is nothing but a combination of excrement from unknown animals.

If you want to make yourself useful, pick one plant—preferably one of their favorites, large and luxuriant—and defecate abundantly next to it. Then shower the surrounding soil generously with your urine, day after day, until you see the plant wither: that is the unequivocal sign that you have done an excellent job. Then move on to the next plant.

Plants that are edible to humans (herbs, attempts at vegetable gardens with tomatoes, and other greens) can be sprinkled directly; more extreme fertilizing techniques involve placing the fecal mass in full view, as a decoration for the leaves and fruits.

When you don't feel like gardening, you can rest by nestling on the smallest and most delicate flowering plants. Crushing them thoroughly makes a very comfortable outdoor bed.

Indulging the human habit of taking care of plant organisms is a noble endeavor, but it is not in our nature. You will therefore inevitably fall prey to moments of murderous attack and won't be able to stop yourself from pouncing on and raging against any form of passive life that happens to be in your way.

Humans may not appreciate that. Make sure you are far removed from the location of the deed when they notice it, and feign indifference.

# Animals

*Dogs are to humans what humans are to cats.*
—Prince Leopoldino

When cohabiting with humans, you may happen to share the territory with other species. What follows is general information. There may be canines deserving of your admiration, friendly parrots, and fish that are larger than you, but those are exceptions.

## Canines

They come in all kinds, shapes, and sizes, from bald ones as small as squirrels to those as large and hairy as bears.

We will be brief: dogs are usually dirty, smelly, noisy, and excessively enthusiastic. They're not nasty—quite the opposite; they're good guys, especially if met on their own. But a little simpleminded. They always cling to humans, never take their eyes off them, and are totally dependent on them. Puppies, particularly if affected by gigantism, are especially clumsy and irritating.

Even so, cohabiting with a dog can be an undoubted source of entertainment. Moreover, some of them have personalities and habits that are more compatible with ours, and it has been proved that they can become excellent friends.

In any case, bring them to heel from the outset.

### Rodents

These are kept in small cages through which you can see them but not reach them. A form of incomprehensible sadism but widely documented. Why imprison them for the whole of their miserable lives when they could give you the job?

### Fish

The same applies to them as to rodents, with the difference that fish are prettier to look at and more mesmerizing. Their cages are glass boxes called aquariums. Keep an eye on the transparency of the water: when it gets dirty, the primate will clean the aquarium and move the fish into a less sophisticated container. That's the time to strike.

### Birds

Here we can see how far human cruelty reaches. Birds are often kept in cages where they cannot even *fly*! It is your moral duty to find any way of opening these cages and putting an end to their misery.

Parrots are a different matter. They are fearsome creatures. First, they are clever. Sometimes, they talk to humans, probably giving them directives. They are ruthless, armed with large bills and talons, and are proud and aggressive: we advise you to keep away from large parrots.

### Reptiles and Amphibians

Incomprehensibly, some humans keep in their territory specimens of these animals—also usually kept shut in transparent glass boxes. We like tortoises very much, and they can be used as vantage points or slow means of transport; you can mess around with their shell or play hide-and-seek with it. Apart from tortoises, other reptiles and amphibians are generally revolting and unworthy of our interest. When large snakes are present and allowed to circulate freely, keep an eye on them and, if possible, move house.

### Other Primates
It is our opinion that all the apes too large to be devoured by a cat are evidently partial to our species.

Despite the fact that there are few opportunities for us to socialize with other primates, fate—usually in human form—sometimes causes it to happen.

There are rumors about a prime example—that of Koko, a gorilla raised in captivity to whom Francine, a human, taught sign language. Even though the two had spent time together for many years, Koko never managed to teach Francine gorilla language—which proves once again how poorly equipped these loquacious animals are to listen. But let us not digress.

What we wish to bring to your attention is that when Francine, using sign language, asked Koko what her greatest wish was, she replied, "A cat." And there are numerous reports about the friendship that bound Koko, throughout her long life, to various cats.

# CONCLUSION

## A HUMAN IS FOREVER

Humans live long. If you have trained your specimen well, it will be yours forever. Even when you are old, toothless, unwilling to eat, and unable to use the toilet with dignity, the ape will continue to serve you and may take you to the Untrainable to prolong your agony.

If you have chosen an animal that enjoys a high social standing and many resources, this will probably happen.

To get it over with, you must agree to urinate pretty much everywhere, even in the king-size bed, and while they are in it. This could, at last, induce them to let you go, albeit with a heavy heart.

This is the paradox of these large mammals: although, as a species, they are frightening, on an individual basis they can be loving, and they know how to be protective, clever, and generous creatures. In their own way, of course—inelegantly, noisily, clumsily—but, just like felines, they ask for nothing but to love and be loved.

# ACKNOWLEDGMENTS

To Daria Bignardi and Giulia Ichino, the first primates to read the manuscript, who believed it could be of interest to other apes. To Andrea Ferolla, whose approval and generosity were essential, and not only because of the wonderful illustrations that subsequently materialized from them. To Annalisa Lottini and the entire Giunti team, who followed and supported me (the way you do with dangerous lunatics). To Gretchen Schmid, who fell in love with the book and took care of the English edition with feline precision and grace. To Katherine Gregor, who has translated my words with humor and elegance into a language I love and would like to know as well as she does. To LeeAnn Bortolussi, who passionately accompanies the book in its new incarnations. To my cat-loving friends, who encouraged and helped me: among them, Margie Gianni, Scott and Lucy Brooker, Giulia and Grazia De Amicis, Cristiana De Rysky, Margherita Ferracuti, Francesca Filiasi, and Renata Orlandini. To my family, who have taught me to love other animals: to my grandmother Wanda, who, before leaving home, would always prepare a small bundle of biscuits she slipped into her handbag in case she came across some of her canine friends; to my father and mother, who taught me to get to know and take care of other living creatures. To my brothers and nephews, who always help and support me. To Andrea Massari, who has been an enthusiastic reader from the outset. Always and as ever, to Stefano Massari, my beloved, who is the best ally one could wish for.

Thank you.

# A NOTE FROM THE TRANSLATOR

I had always wanted to translate a book involving animals—even better if the narrator was an animal. I am an animal lover. Moreover, an unapologetic anthropomorphist. As far as I am concerned, anything that makes humans more empathic toward their fellow earthlings is a good thing, and if that entails attributing human thoughts and emotions to birds, mammals, and reptiles, then so be it. After all, the sensibilities and ponderings we imagine in animals tend to be much finer than those in humans. In our fiction, animals are often craftier, truer, and wiser than humans, and are endowed with an insight we, sadly, lack.

I was raised on the fairy tales of Alexander Afanasyev: talking bears, prophetic frogs, cunning vixens, loyal eagles, and wise wolves. The first book I ever translated from Italian was Pino Cacucci's *The Whales Know*.

When I heard that HarperVia had acquired the rights to Babas's *Come addomesticare un umano*, I practically begged to translate it. Here was not only a book written from the point of view of an animal, but one of the cleverest, most perceptive, and mysterious animals: the cat. Cats, as many of us know, are superior creatures who know they are superior. You can tell by the self-possessed expression in their luminous eyes. An expression that cuts you down to size, puts you in your place, and warns you not to think too highly of yourself.

In *How to Train Your Human*, Babas captures the tone of the cat exactly as we imagine it would be if we were evolved enough to understand cat language. She pays tribute to the cat's elegance, insightfulness, majesty, shrewdness, adaptability—and ruthlessness. Anyone who has ever been fortunate enough to share their living quarters with a cat will agree that their friendship is hard to earn and, once obtained, is an honor and a joy. In *How to Train Your Human*, Babas uses her sharp humor but also great warmth to lead us into the inner mental life of cats as we perceive and experience it, and also provides a healthy dose of human self-deprecation. Yes, we apes have so much to learn. I do not often have the good fortune to burst out laughing while translating: thank you, Babas and Gretchen Schmid at Harper-Via, for this precious gift.

The author dedicated her book to the cats who have been a part of her life. I wish to dedicate this translation to the memory of Pyewacket and Genie, my darling feline witches—and to the cats to come.

—Katherine Gregor

## A NOTE FROM THE ILLUSTRATOR

I thought I was a cat, then I read the manuscript of this book and realized that *she*—Babas—was the cat.

I decided to accompany this highly stylish manual with quick, broad, deep-black strokes. In my study in Rome, I made Loulou, Pastis, Thelma, and Louise pose for me, but they kept moving. I filled sheets and sheets of paper with doodles and slashes of ink, trying to capture a feline expression, pose, or leap.

After a while, I became very fast and was able to deliver the plates for the print.

I now keep the book on my nightstand, and my cats also glance at it every now and then. They read it and look at me, and I get the sense they are laughing at me among themselves.

—Andrea Ferolla

Ferolla

Here ends Baba's
*How to Train Your Human.*

The first edition of the book was printed
and bound at Lakeside Book Company
in Harrisonburg, Virginia, April 2024.

A NOTE ON THE TYPE

This book was set in Arno Pro, a sturdy serif font created by the American designer Robert Slimbach. Its name comes from the river that runs through Florence, a center of the Italian Renaissance. Slimbach was principally inspired by Renaissance-era typography in creating the Arno typeface, but adjusted the design and kerning of those early designs to be crisper and more readable for this contemporary update. Its Italian-inspired charm and quiet elegance make it an ideal fit for *How to Train Your Human.*

**HARPERVIA**

An imprint dedicated to publishing international voices,
offering readers a chance to encounter other lives and other
points of view via the language of the imagination.